Take a P I C C

P onder

I nspect

C hange Essential Settings

C apture

A Guide to Snapping Pictures with
any Camera or Phone

Reid Brown

What others have said about Take a PICC

“A quick and easy guide to seeing the photo
before you even take it”

- Independent Book Review -

Take a PICC: A Guide to Snapping Pictures with Any Camera or Phone.

Cover design by Reid Brown.

Table of Contents

Introduction

Hello, this book came into being through a desire to help those interested learn the art of seeing creatively using any camera or phone, based on my personal experiences as a self-taught artist.

My journey began when I was 12, using a Panasonic 4 mega pixel camera to snap pictures of my pets, birds in my family's pond, flowers, and the stream near our property. Experimenting with different picture-framing compositions, I progressed through practice and learning from my mistakes to where I am today on my own picture taking trek.

Throughout the book, I have included relevant insights and a few of the mistakes I made that are related to each subject being discussed that I learned on that journey.

I empathize with any potential frustration as I have been there myself while learning to take pictures. However, I encourage you not to give up, as I have faith in your ability to develop your own way of seeing creatively through a camera lens.

Contrary to most photography how-to books that focus on technical camera concepts first. This book follows the creative process P.I.C.C..

In P.I.C.C., the introductory spotlight is instead on developing an understanding of creative composition before going over essential camera settings, related concepts surrounding those settings and touching any gear. This reversed approach outlined below will help you comfortably take pictures with any camera or phone.

Ponder: Explore a calming, meditative technique to help you focus your attention on the subject you wish to photograph.

Inspect: Master the art of arranging the subject and supporting objects within a scene using the following concepts:

> Rule of thirds and fill the frame composition principles.
>
> Elements of design in composition: line, shape, form, texture, color and space.

Change essential settings: Gain insight into and adjust the essential camera settings and surrounding concepts, listed below, to enhance the subject of interest.

> Shutter speed, exposure triangle, ISO, aperture, and depth of field.

Capture: Put it all together and use your new skills to confidently capture priceless moments with more creativity.

After reading this book be more creatively confident while taking a P.I.C.C.!

Ponder

Look and think before opening the shutter. The heart and mind are the true lens of the camera.

- Yousuf Karsh -

Before you begin reflecting on your picture, take a moment to settle your mind by trying some aspects of the calming 5-4-3-2-1 grounding technique described below. This practice gently guides your attention to become aware of your immediate surroundings and senses.

Look around and focus on an object that draws your attention. [1]

Listen and focus on a sound you hear. [1]

Concentrate upon your chosen sound and object with curiosity while taking deep breaths for a couple of minutes, easing your mind into a more relaxed state. [1]

I first tried this grounding technique at Chiricahua National Monument in southeast Arizona. I had planned the picture ahead of time and woke up at 4:30am to capture the sunrise. Being present and connected to the landscape made the photograph more meaningful to me.

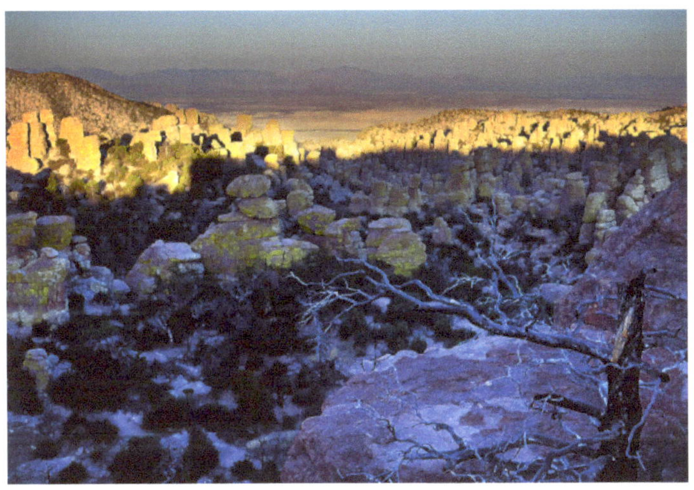

Chiricahua National Monument. Reid Brown, 2018.

Chapter Notes

1. "Exploring Mindfulness and the 5-4-3-2-1 Grounding Activity ::
Lincolnshire Young Minds," January 10, 2022. https://www.lpft.nhs.
uk/young-people/lincolnshire/about-us/whats-new/grounding-activity.

Inspect

Composition

After relaxing your mind, admire the scene. Identify the subject you want to take a picture of and any objects that surround it.

Take a moment, write them down.

For now, hold off on getting out that camera or opening the camera app. Focus on grasping the concepts presented. *Composition* refers to the way you position the objects and subject within the frame such that your photograph tells the story or conveys the message you want it to. [1]

While there are no strict rules for composing a photograph, using the two principles below can be helpful tools to achieving your own, unique creative eye in taking pictures.

The *rule of thirds* reference places a subject to the left or right of the frame, offset from the center. [1]

Filling the frame refers to capturing a scene where the subject and supporting objects dominate the majority of the frame, ensuring that the viewer's attention is focused on them. [2]

While there are multiple composition techniques, the two above have helped me establish my own creative eye with practice.

Create a frame with your hands and visualize a grid within it, as shown on the next page. Place your subject and objects within this hand-frame. This grid helps you draw attention to your subject and achieve visual balance when using your hand-frame and later your phone or camera.

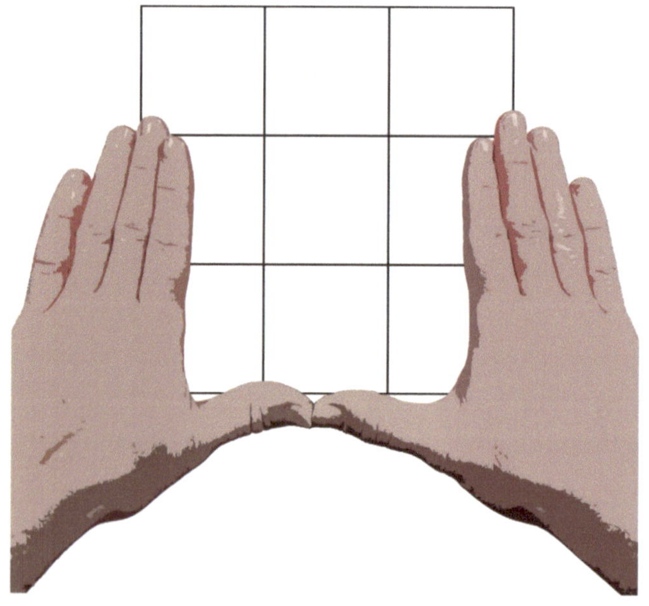

Hand-Frame. Reid Brown, 2023.

Now let's look at some examples to help with the concept of composition. When observing the following pictures, imagine framing the scenes using the hand-frame approach.

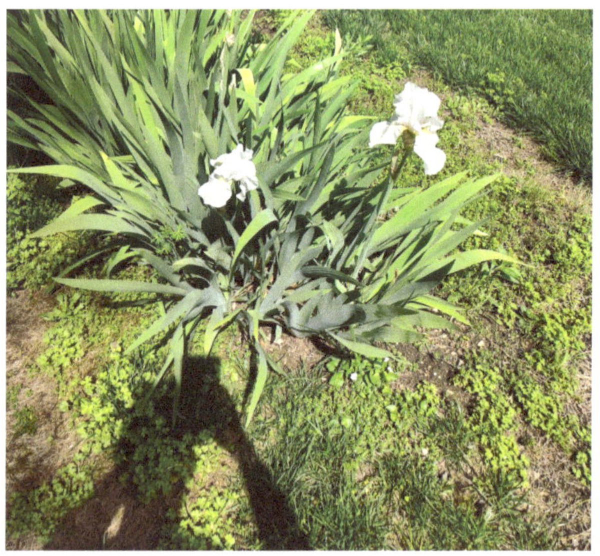

Iris A. Reid Brown, 2023.

Objects: *grass, flower blades and shadow.*
Subject: *flower.*

With so many natural details present, the image generates a visual complexity that makes it challenging to focus solely on the primary subject—the flowers. The viewer's gaze shifts to the surrounding objects, such as the grass in the foreground and the shadow cast across the frame. As a result, the abundance of objects within the scene scatters attention and makes it difficult for the eye to settle on a single focal point. On the next page, we will move the frame closer to the subject to reduce these distractions.

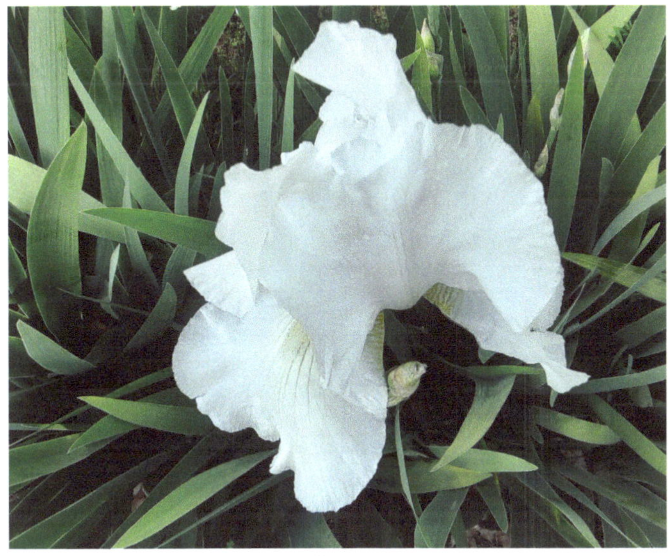

Iris B. Reid Brown, 2023.

Objects: *flower blades.*
Subject: *flower.*

After re-positioning the frame in the scene and applying both the rule of thirds and fill-the-frame principles to keep the subject off-center, some objects have been removed to clarify the subject for the viewer. Additionally, the flower blades now visually balance the flower within the framed scene.

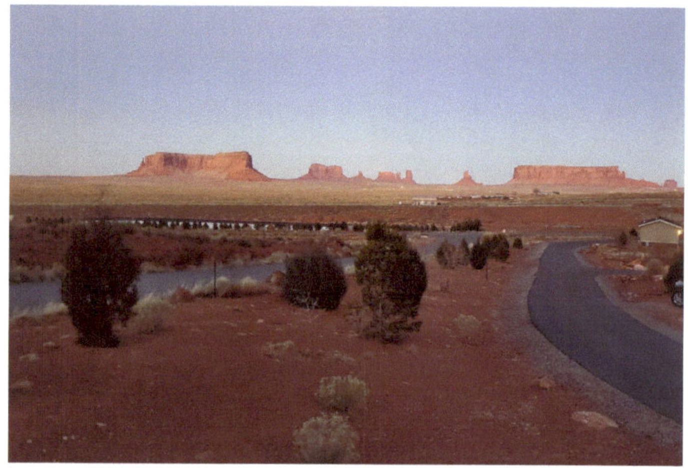

Mesa. Reid Brown, 2018.

Objects: *red soil, bushes, road.*
Subject: *mesa in background..*

The abundance of visual elements in the foreground—such as the
vivid red soil, scattered bushes, and winding road—introduces a
sense of visual complexity that competes for the viewer's attention.
Rather than allowing the eye to naturally settle on the mesa in the
distance, these foreground objects draw focus in multiple
directions across the scene. This dispersal of attention makes it
difficult for the intended subject to stand out as the central focal
point. On the opposite page, we will shift the framing, guiding the
viewer more directly toward the mesa.

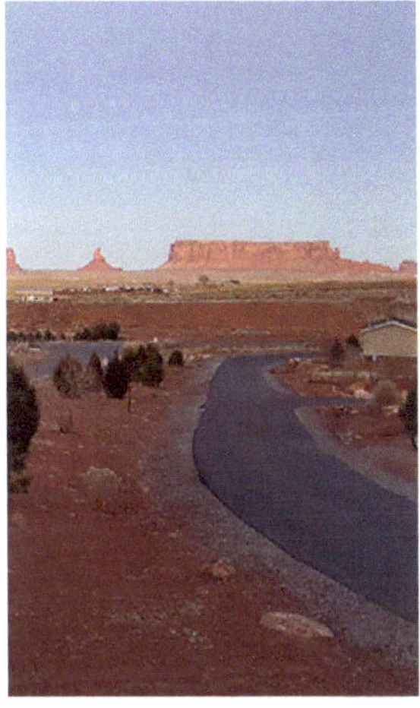
Mesa. Reid Brown, 2018.

Objects: *red soil, road.*
Subject: *mesa in background.*

After shifting the frame to another position and eliminating some distracting objects, the road now occupies a larger portion of the foreground. It is slightly offset from the center, following the rule of thirds principle. This guides the viewer's attention toward the mesa in the background, with the road serving as a visual pathway.

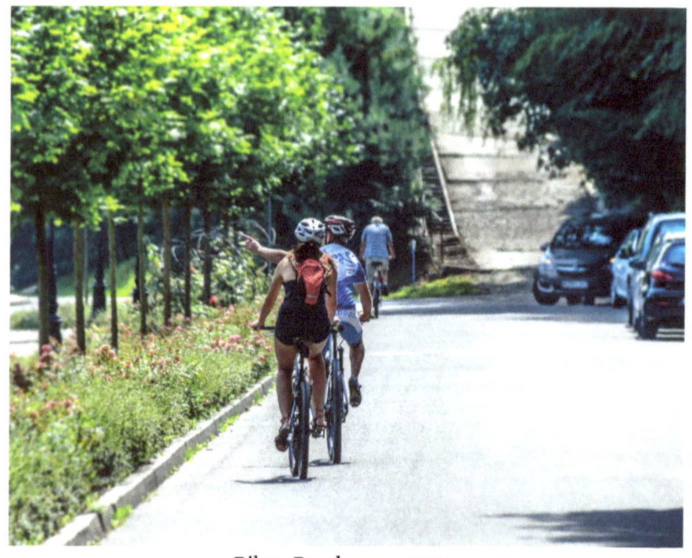

Bikes. Pexels.com, 2023.

Objects: *row of trees, street, cars.*
Subject: *people on bicycles.*

This broad framed image, though rich in detail, creates visual complexity that makes it difficult to focus on a single subject, such as the two people on bikes. The viewer's attention is pulled to various objects and figures across the image, dispersing focus instead of settling on a central point. On the next page, we'll move the frame closer to the subject.

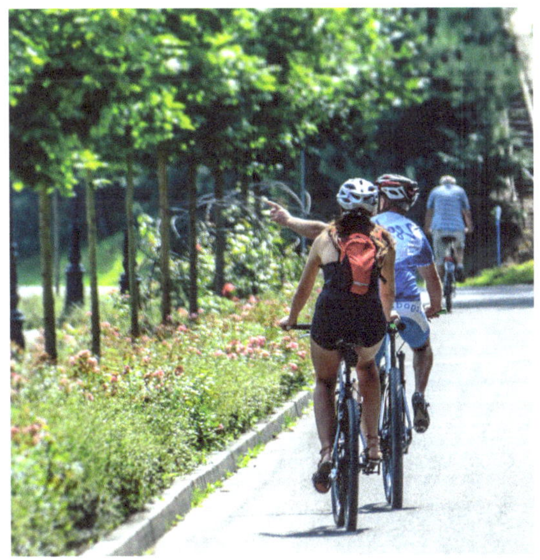

Bikes. Pexels.com, 2023.

Objects: *row of trees and flowers, road.*
Subject: *people on bicycles.*

By moving the frame closer to the bikers, the focus centers on them, with previously noticeable objects like cars now out of view. This directs the viewer's attention to the cyclists and their interaction, resulting in a more intimate and dynamic scene.

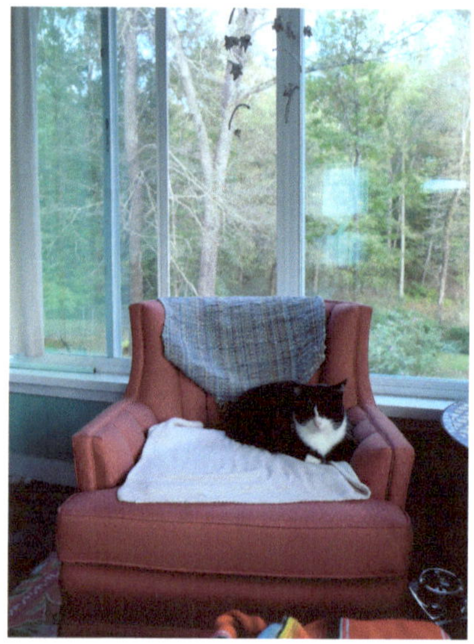

Earl the cat. Reid Brown, 2011.

Objects: *red blanket, side table, pink chair, trees in background.*
Subject: *Earl the cat.*

Now, take a look at the final example. Notice how the visual clutter in the room pulls your attention away from the main subject. The objects surrounding the chair distract from where your focus should be—Earl laying on the chair. On the next page, we'll bring the frame in closer and simplify the scene.

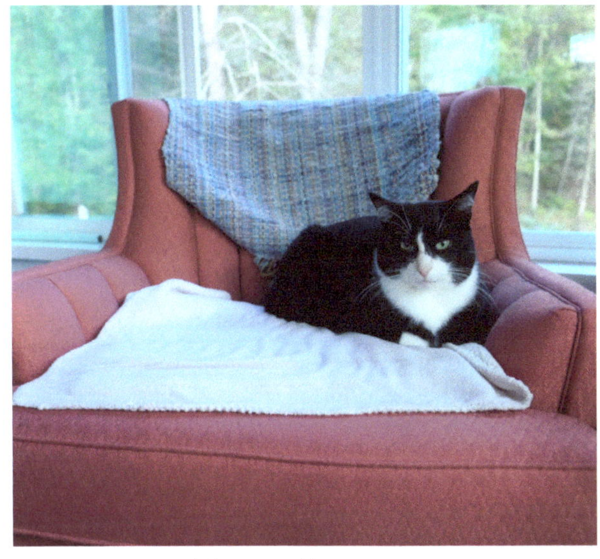

Earl the cat. Reid Brown, 2011.

Objects: *pink chair, trees in background.*
Subject: *Earl the cat.*

By moving in closer and simplifying the scene, Earl becomes the clear focal point. Positioning him off-center using the rule of thirds naturally attracts attention, while allowing both Earl and the chair to fill more of the frame, enhancing the sense of his presence and personality.

Go ahead and frame your subject and supporting objects in your hand-frame again. Then, practice their compositional placement using the rule of thirds and fill the frame principles you have observed in the examples provided on the previous pages.

Need some extra practice? Scan the QR code below, when the website opens search for your favorite subject or place and find pictures that utilize the composition principles presented.

Through my experiences capturing scenes, whether using the hand-frame concept, camera, or smartphone, I've found it's beneficial to keep the number of objects to a minimum. This helps guide the viewer's focus to the intended subject and balances the subject visually. Also, I encourage you to not be afraid of holding any device you use to take pictures at different angles, like laying down for example. This adds a creative uniqueness to your compositions.

Chapter Notes

1. Adobe. "The Basics of Photography Composition | Adobe," n.d. https://www.adobe.com/creativecloud/photography/discover/photo-composition.html.

2. "What Is Fill the Frame Photography? - Adobe." Accessed August 17, 2023. https://www.adobe.com/creativecloud/photography/hub/guides/fill-the-frame-photography.html.

Inspect

Elements of Design in Composition

Think of the objects in your framed scene now as elements of design. There are several types:

Space, form, texture, shape, line, and color. [1]

Let's look at each in more detail. Again, imagine framing the pictures using the hand-frame method.

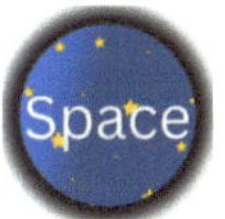

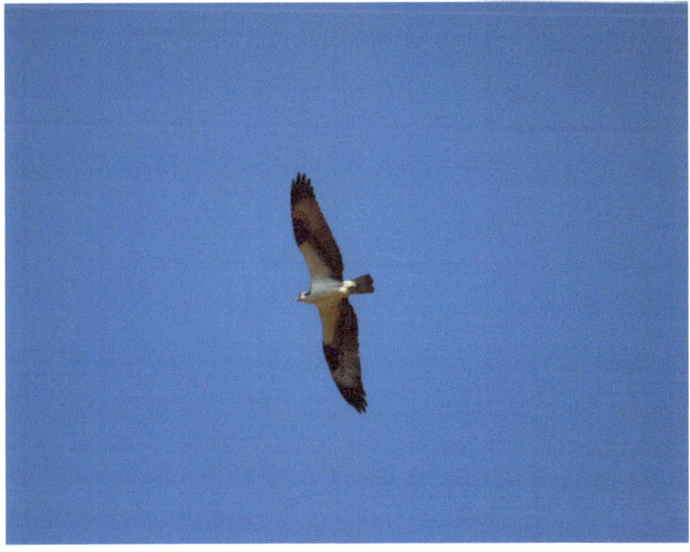

Osprey. Reid Brown, 2015.

Space is the area around and between the elements of design and subject. Here, it is the blue sky surrounding an osprey.

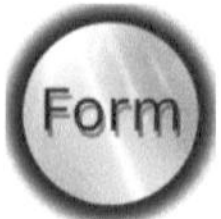

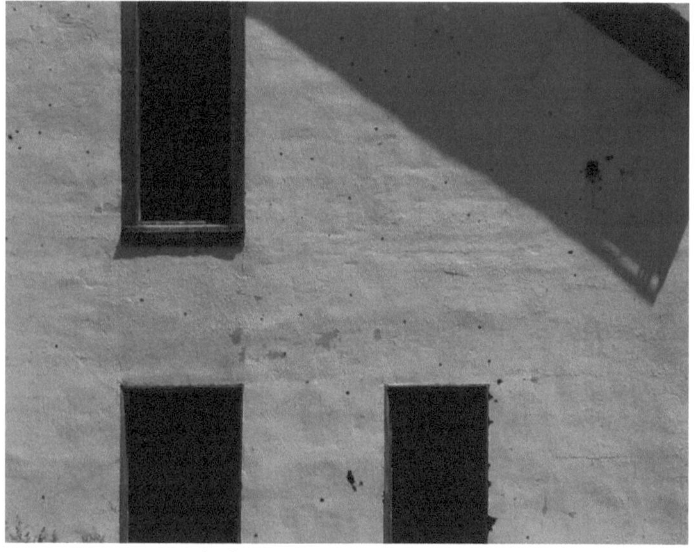

Shadow House. Reid Brown, 2015.

Form is any 3-D aspect of a framed scene. The shadow formed by a building roof line is an example of form.

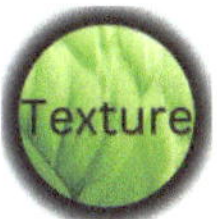

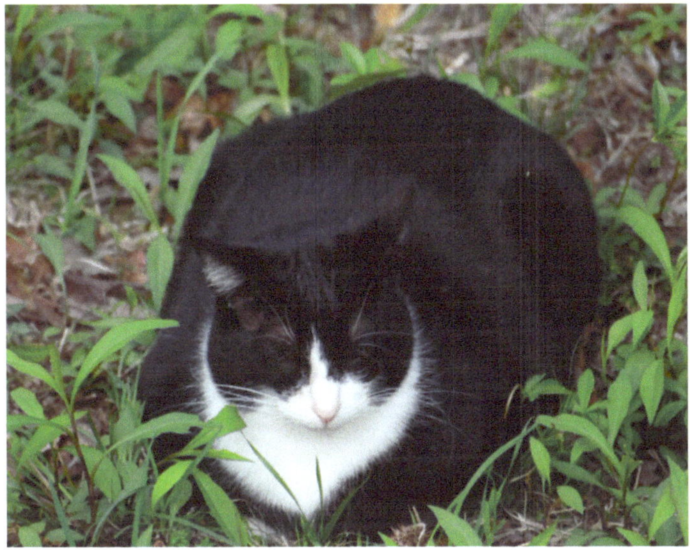

Earl. Reid Brown, 2015.

Texture refers to a surface quality of objects. In this picture, the grass surrounding Earl is the texture adding visual balance.

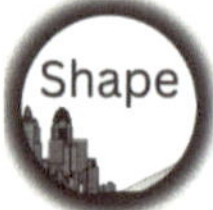

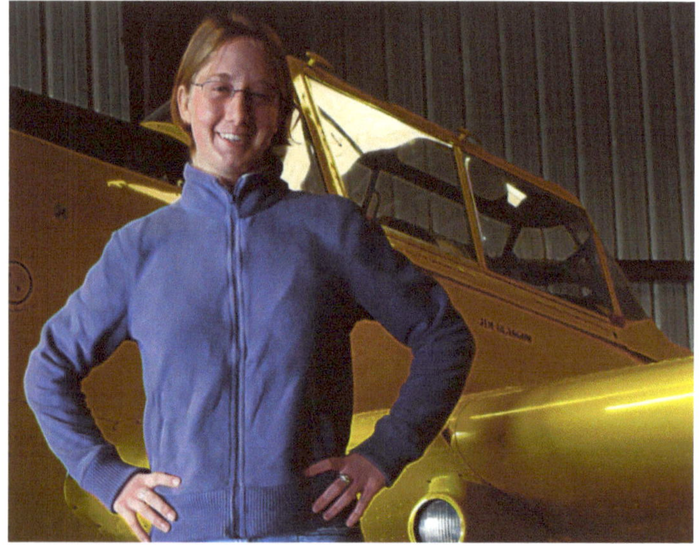

The Aviator. Reid Brown, 2007.

Shape is an object or combination of different lines. It can be
used to tell a story about the subject. Here, the airplane behind
the subject displays her interest in this activity.

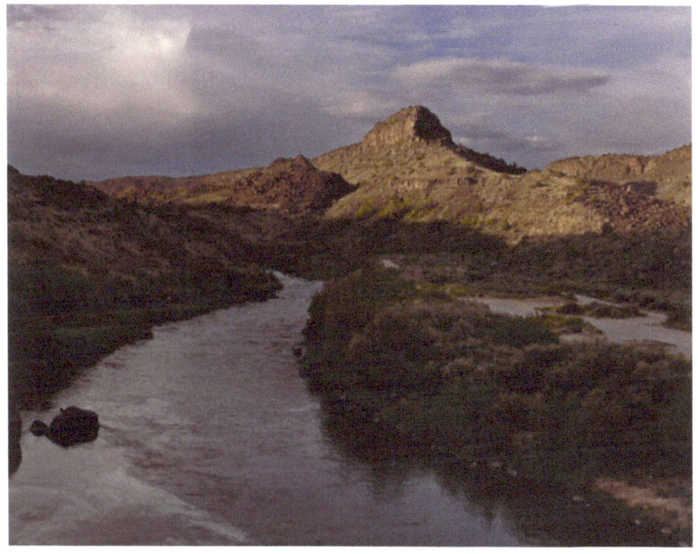

Rio Grande. Reid Brown, 2010.

Line is any straight, curved, diagonal or implied line that leads a viewer to a subject. In this photo, the river leads the viewer to a distant mountain.

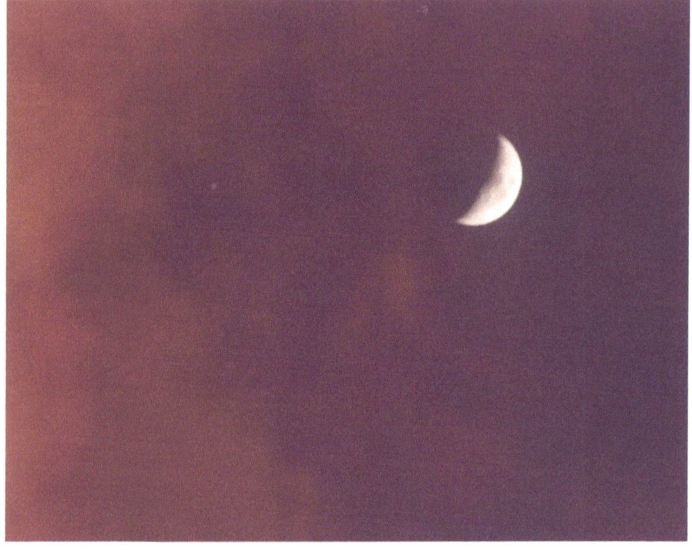

Moon and Clouds. Reid Brown, 2008.

Color: adds emotion to a framed scene. Different colors can evoke different feelings. Here we see an orange-colored lit sky visually balancing the moon. As another example, when taking portrait pictures, have the subject wear their favorite color, which can show the person's unique energy.

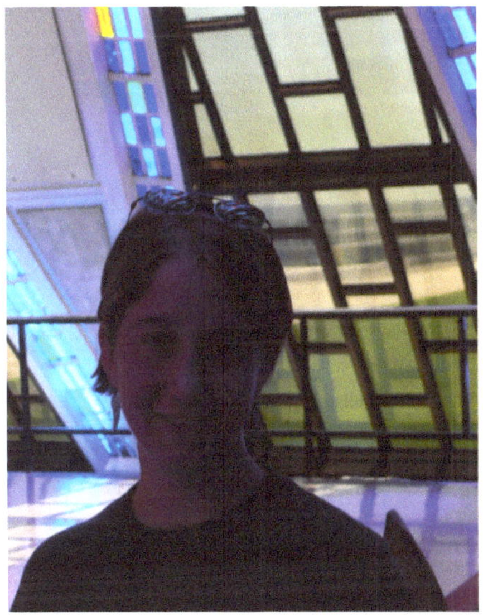

Church. Reid Brown, 2010.

When I began learning about the elements of design, I discovered that using colors brighter than the subject in a picture can mislead viewers, as shown in the image above.

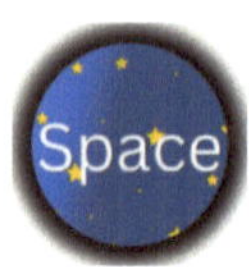

The area around a subject.

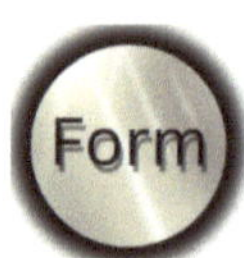

Any 3-D aspect of a framed scene. The shadow created by a building roof line is an example of form.

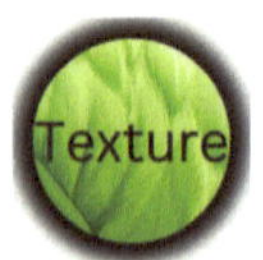

A surface quality of objects. Some examples: bushes or grass.

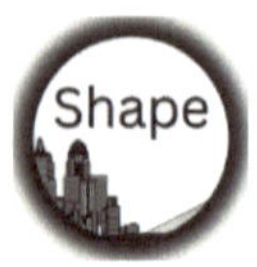

An object or combination of different lines, can be used to tell a story about the subject.

Any straight, curved, diagonal, or implied line that leads a viewer to a subject.

Adds emotion to a framed scene. Different colors can evoke different feelings.

Thinking back to the objects you wrote down earlier, what elements of design could they be replaced with?

I encourage you to be creative and combine any of the elements of design to best highlight the framed subject. Just remember to not overwhelm the viewer, so they can identify your subject.

Need some extra practice? Scan the QR code below, when the website opens search for your favorite subject or place and identify what elements are used to visually draw attention to the subject.

Chapter Notes

1. The Kennedy Center. "Formal Visual Analysis: The Elements & Principles of Composition." The Kennedy Center, n.d. https://www.kennedy-center.org/education/resources-for-educators/classroom-resources/articles-and-how-tos/articles/educators/visual-arts/formal-visual-analysis-the-elements-and-principles-of-compositoin/.

Change Essential Settings

Camera Body Anatomy

What is a camera?

A camera is a box, made to prevent light from entering except through a small opening. This opening allows light to be focused onto a film or sensor that is sensitive to that light, and this creates a picture.

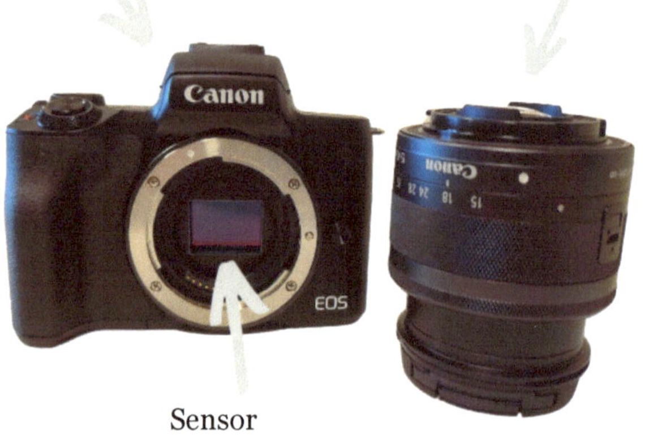

Camera Body. Reid Brown, 2023

The camera is an instrument that teaches people
how to see without a camera.

- Dorothea Lange -

Change Essential Settings

Exposure Triangle

In the following sections, we will look at the essential camera settings and associated concepts:

Exposure triangle, shutter speed, ISO, aperture, and depth of field.

The amount of light entering the camera through the lens is called *exposure.* There are three factors that affect exposure:

shutter speed, ISO, and *aperture.* [1]

These three factors make up what is called the *exposure triangle.*[1]

To change the lighting of a framed scene, or how the viewers see the subject and the elements of design, change the factors of the exposure triangle.

These factors have a direct relationship with each other. This means that when one factor is altered, it has an impact on the other two factors. After each factor is explained we will explore some examples to demonstrate how their proportional relationship works.

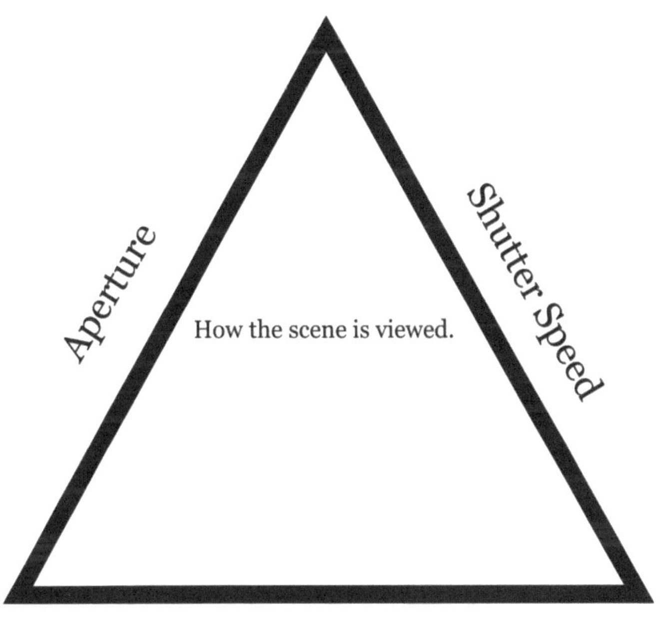

Exposure Triangle. Reid Brown, 2023.

Chapter Notes

1. Vorenkamp, Todd. "Understanding Exposure, Part 1: The Exposure Triangle | B&H EXplora," January 26, 2022. https://www.bhphotovideo.com/explora/photography/tips-and-solutions/understanding-exposure-part-1-exposure-triangle.

Change Essential Settings

Shutter Speed

Shutter speed is the speed of the shutter or "door" in front of the camera sensor. It uses a fraction scale. On any camera or phone you will find it displayed as: S (1/50) or S 50 and so on.[1]

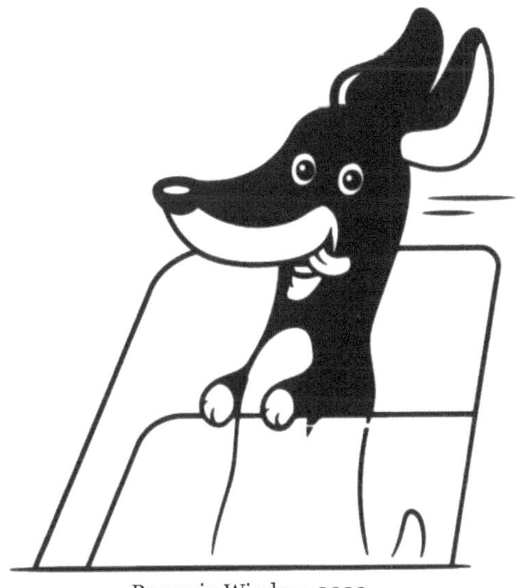

Puppy in Window. 2023.

A fast shutter speed (S 200) will freeze movement within a
framed scene. Like a puppy in a car moving past your camera,
as shown in the graphic above.

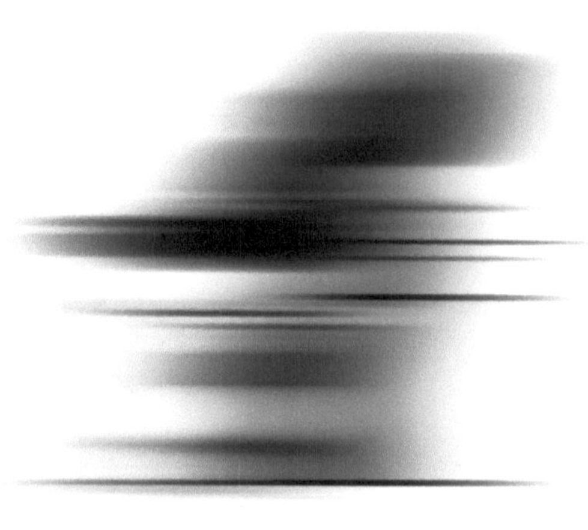

Puppy in Window. 2023.

A slow shutter speed (S 1/3) will blur movement within a framed scene. Like a puppy in a car moving past your camera, as shown in the graphic above.

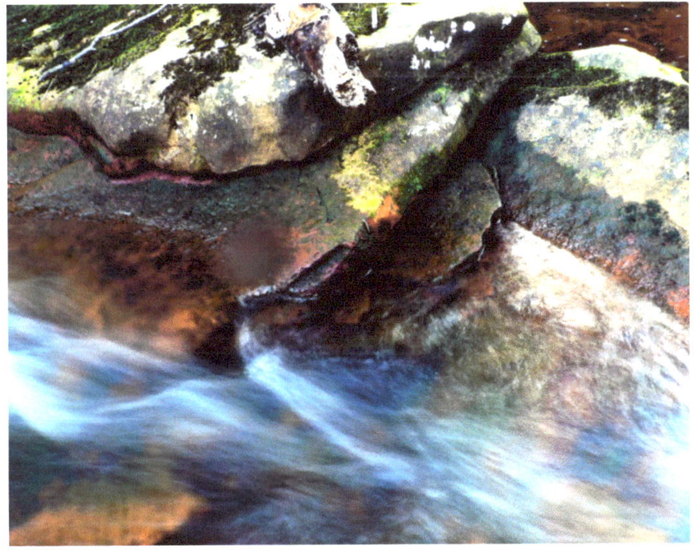

Untitled. Reid Brown, 2006.

Shutter speed and keeping the lighting of the picture where I wanted was a challenge for me when I first started my interest in photography. Then, I really didn't understand how the factors of the exposure triangle affected each other.

Chapter Notes

1. Vorenkamp, Todd. "Understanding Exposure, Part 3: Shutter Speed | B&H EXplora," October 20, 2018. https://www.bhphotovideo.com/explora/photography/tips-and-solutions/understanding-exposure-part-3-shutter-speed.

Change Essential Settings

ISO

ISO is a measure of how sensitive your camera's sensor is to light. On any camera or phone, you will find ISO displayed as ISO LO, ISO 100 and so on. [1]

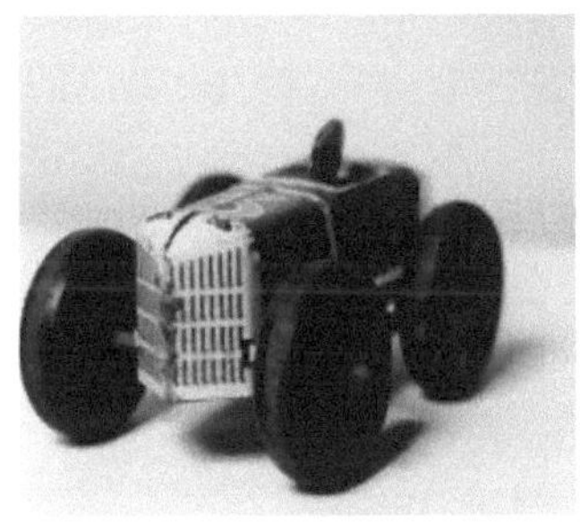

Car. Reid Brown, 2023.

ISO 160

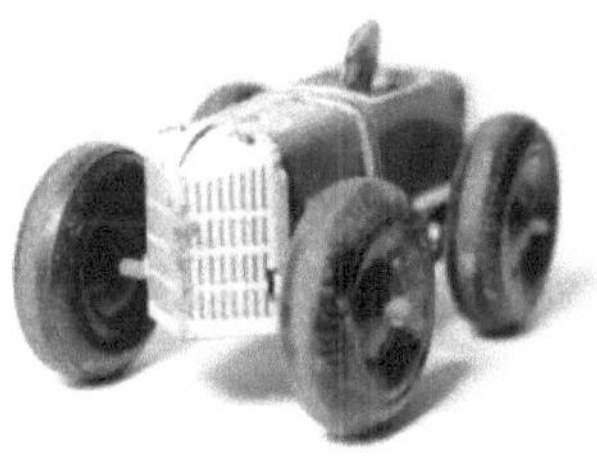

Car. Reid Brown, 2023.

ISO 640

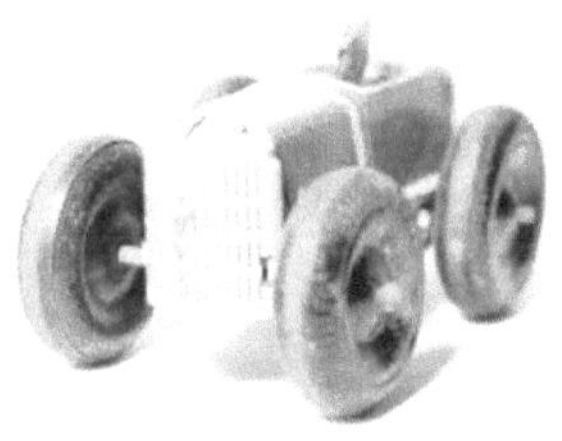

Car. Reid Brown, 2023.

ISO 1250

As seen above, the higher the ISO value, the more sensitive the camera's sensor is to light and the brighter the picture will be.

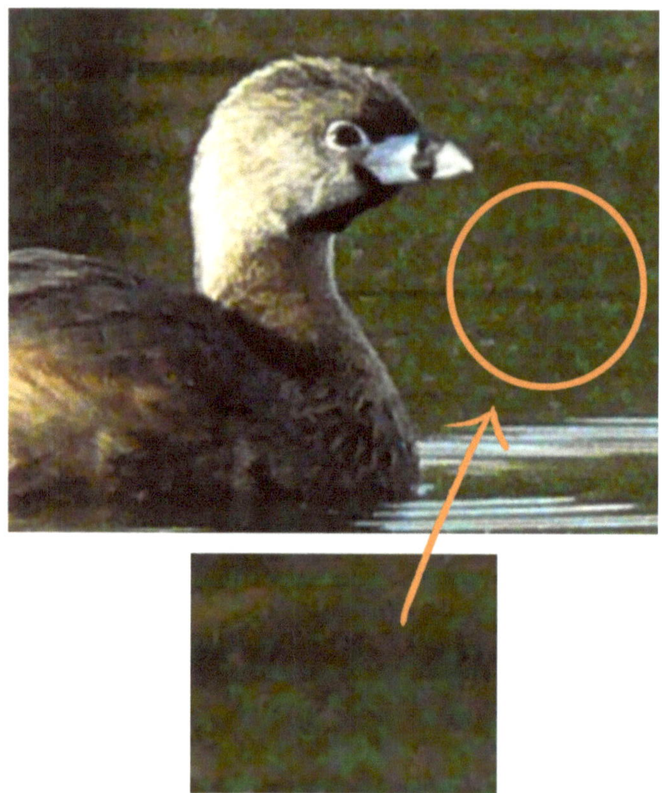

Grebe. Reid Brown, 2007.

An ISO value that is too high can granulate your picture, as seen above. For the best picture quality, try to keep the ISO value as low as possible.

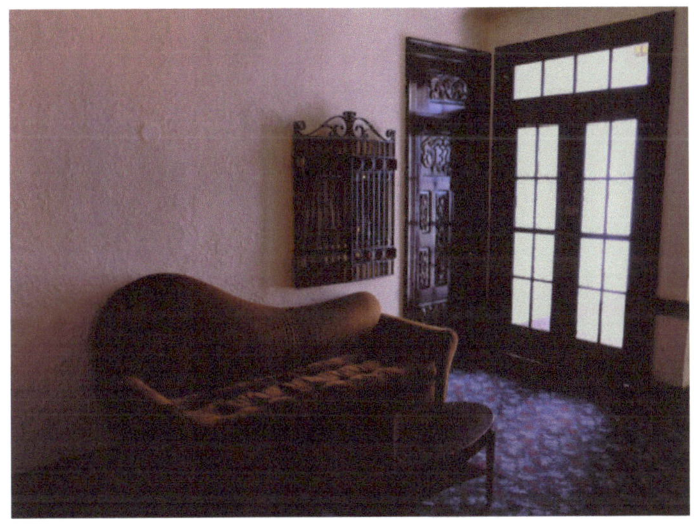

Hotel. Douglas, AZ. Reid Brown, 2016.

I found that when taking pictures inside, it can be beneficial to have a higher ISO value set. This decreases blur from a slower shutter speed when holding the camera by hand. Before going to the picture location, It's handy to know the maximum or brightest ISO value on your camera you can set before the picture gets grainy.

Chapter Notes

1. Vorenkamp, Todd. "Understanding Exposure, Part 4: ISO | B&H EXplora," October 10, 2018. https://www.bhphotovideo.com/explora/photography/tips-and-solutions/understanding-exposure-part-4-iso.

Change Essential Settings

Aperture & Depth of Field

Aperture is a variable opening built within a camera lens. This opening is made using blades that open and close. Shown in the picture below.

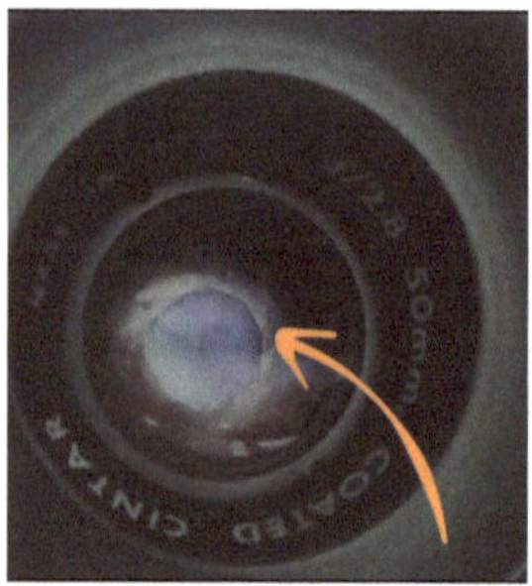

Aperture . Reid Brown, 2023.

This opening affects two things:

How much light that enters the camera.

Depth of field, which is how much of your framed scene is in focus. [1]

Aperture uses a fractional ratio called *F / Stop.* [1]

Where *F* represents the lens *focal length.* Focal length is the optical distance from the point where light rays meet inside the lens to the camera sensor. The camera diagram on the opposite page displays this visually. [2]

Any number after the F is the obtained value from dividing the lens focal length by the diameter of the aperture opening in the lens. [1]

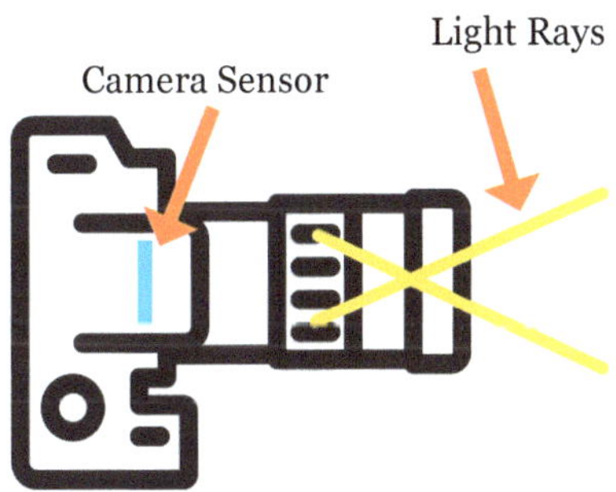

Focal Length. Reid Brown, 2023.

The word *stop* originates to a time when photographers used something called a Waterhouse stop. This was a set of metal plates with different sized holes that would slide in front of the lens, see picture below. The Waterhouse stop is a predecessor to apertures we see in cameras today. [3]

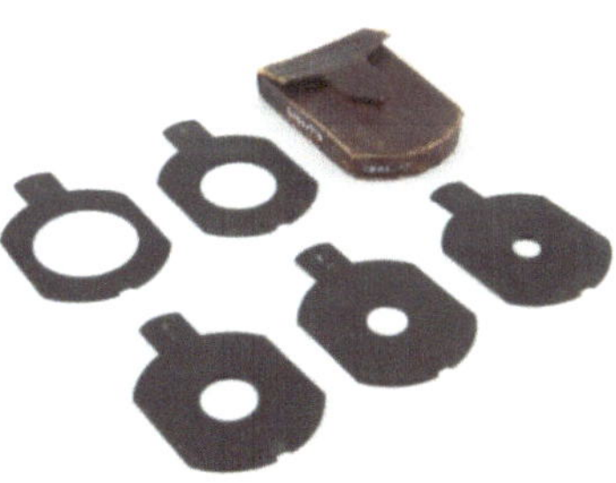

Waterhouse Stops. Science Museum Group Collective, n.d. [3]

As of 2023, most cell phones don't have actual aperture blades inside the lens. An exception to this would be cell phones like the Huawei Mate 50 Pro. On any camera and some cell phones you will find aperture and its F / Stop scale displayed as: F2.5, F4, F6.3, F 11 and so on. The fraction symbol is understood and not shown. On the following page we will look at some examples.

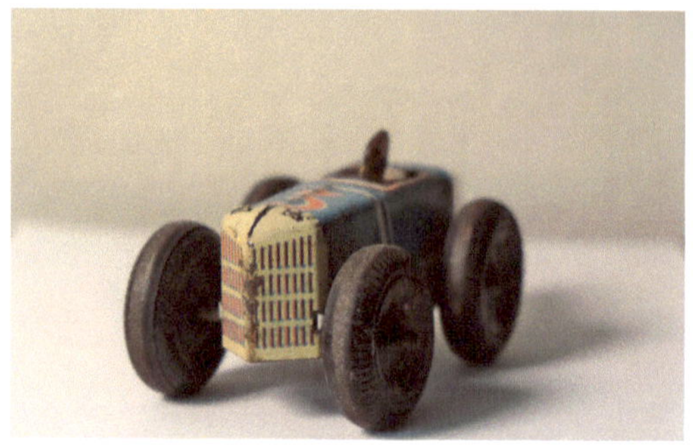

Car. Reid Brown, 2023. Aperture set to (F 3).

An (F 3) aperture has a narrow depth of field, meaning only a small section of the car above is in focus.

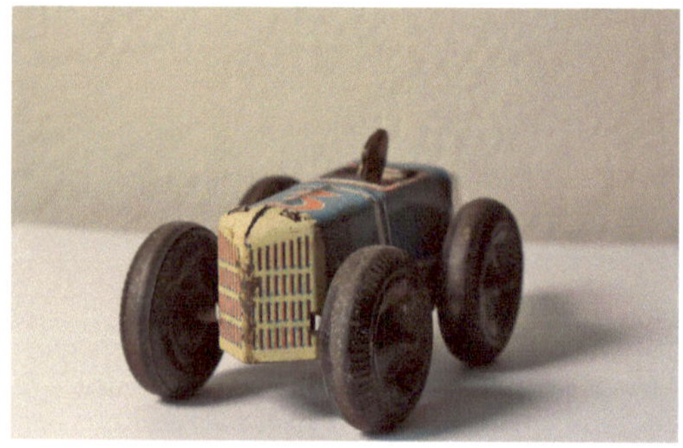

Car. Reid Brown, 2023. Aperture set to (F 6).

An (F 6) aperture has a medium depth of field, so a larger section of the car above is in focus.

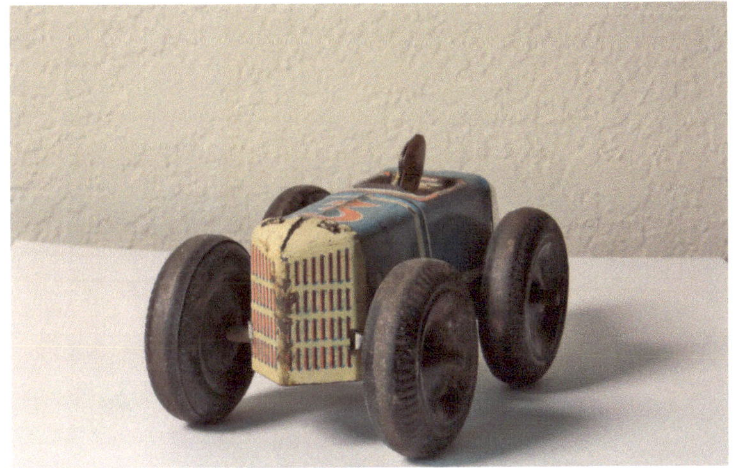

Car. Reid Brown, 2023. Aperture set to (F 10).

An (F 10) aperture has a large depth of field, meaning most of the car and background is in focus, as seen above.

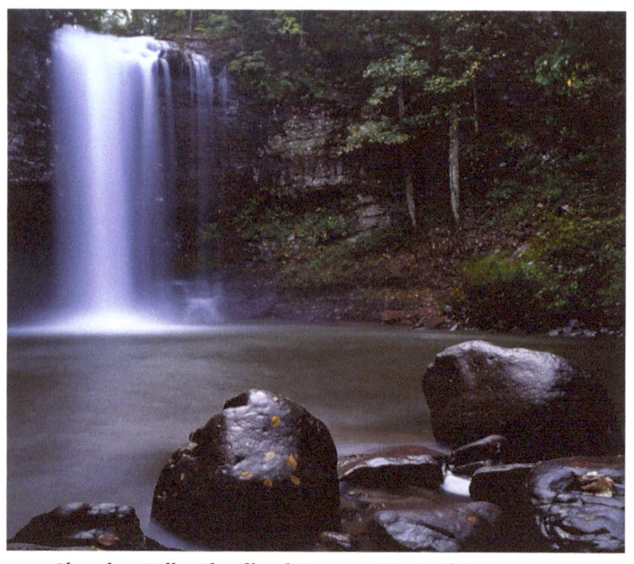

Cherokee Falls. Cloudland Canyon, GA. Reid Brown, 2021.

When I capture landscape scenes, I typically set my aperture close to (F 8) to acquire a picture that has a broad depth of field. On the other side of the aperture spectrum, when snapping portrait pictures, I typically adjust my aperture to around (F 4) in order to emphasize the subject and create a blurred background.

Look at you, you now understand the foundations of photography
That is awesome!

Chapter Notes

1. Petrella, Brenda. "What Is Aperture in Photography? Key Concepts Explained." Outdoor Photography School, January 16, 2020. https://www.outdoorphotographyschool.com/what-is-aperture-in-photography/.

2. "Focal Length | Understanding Camera Zoom & Lens Focal Length | Nikon | Nikon." Accessed November 15, 2023. https://www.nikonusa.com/en/learn-and-explore/a/tips-and-techniques/understanding-focal-length.html.

3. "Waterhouse Stops | Science Museum Group Collection." Accessed November 16, 2023. https://collection.sciencemuseumgroup.org.uk/objects/co8411680/waterhouse-stops-shutter.

Change Essential Settings

Examples

When changing the factors of the exposure triangle, I answer the questions below to best highlight my subject and the elements of design.

Do I want my picture to be in focus across a majority of the scene or to be blurry and have a small area in focus?

Is there movement in the scene, will the subject and elements of design be blurry or focused?

Again, when tweaking ISO, keep it set at its lowest value or just before the picture starts to get grainy for those low light or indoor scenes. On the following few pages we will go over some visual examples to help build an understanding of the proportional relationship of these factors.

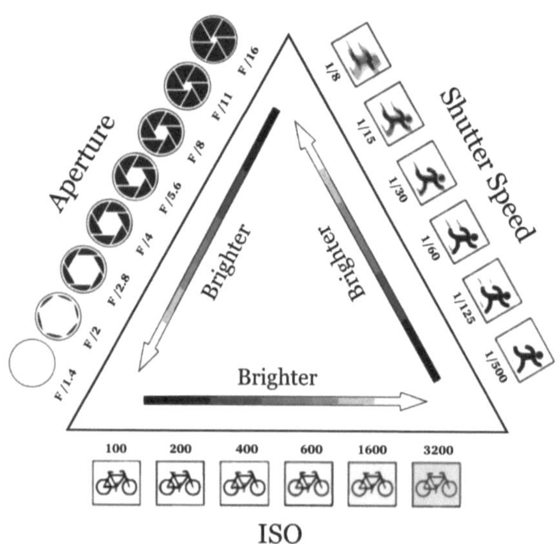

Exposure Triangle. Action Camera Blog, 2017. [1]

To make a scene in focus across a majority of the frame using a camera, shown in the pictures below. First, set aperture to a higher value (F 8) and leave it set. This will darken the scene and help most of the frame be in focus. Secondly, adjust the shutter speed value to the exposure that attracts your creative liking. For my picture below I felt creatively comfortable with my shutter speed set to (S 30). Take a look at the bottom picture to see how the higher aperture adds more focus to the scene.

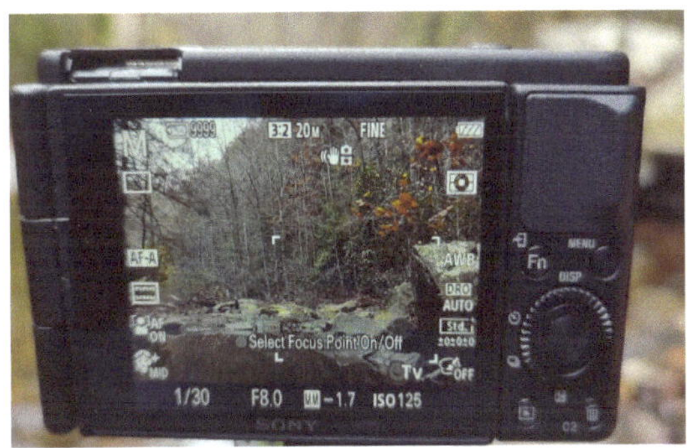

Stream A. Reid Brown, 2023.

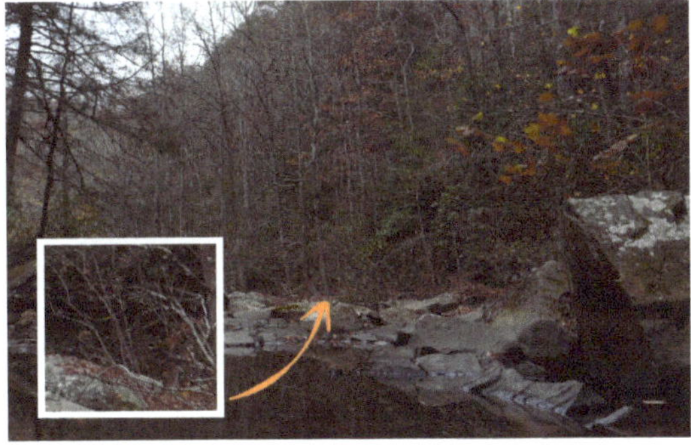

Stream B. Reid Brown , 2023.

To make a scene in focus across a majority of the frame using a cell phone, observe the pictures below. First, to adjust the following settings go to pro mode in the phone app. Secondly, set your ISO to auto. Lastly, adjust shutter speed to the exposure that you enjoy. For my picture below I liked my shutter speed set to (S 45). Because I don't have a cell phone with an adjustable aperture the scene will automatically be sharp across the scene. My cell phones aperture is set permanently to a low value during the manufacturing process.

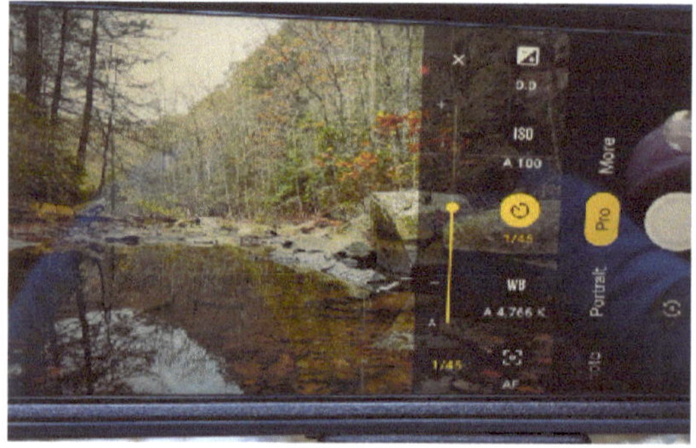

Stream C. Reid Brown , 2023.

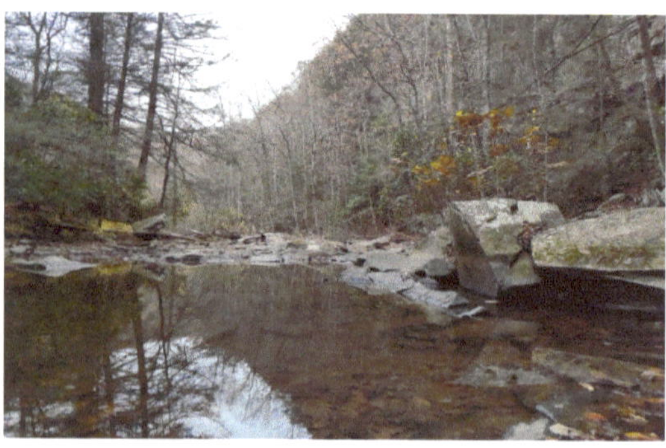

Stream D. Reid Brown , 2023.

To make a scene blurry and have a small area in focus using a camera, observe the pictures below. First, set aperture to a lower value (F 3.5) and leave it set. This will brighten the scene and help only your subject be in focus. Secondly, adjust shutter speed value to the exposure that you find pleasing. For my picture below I felt creatively comfortable with my shutter speed set to (S 20). Take a look at the bottom picture to see how the lower aperture adds more blur to the scene.

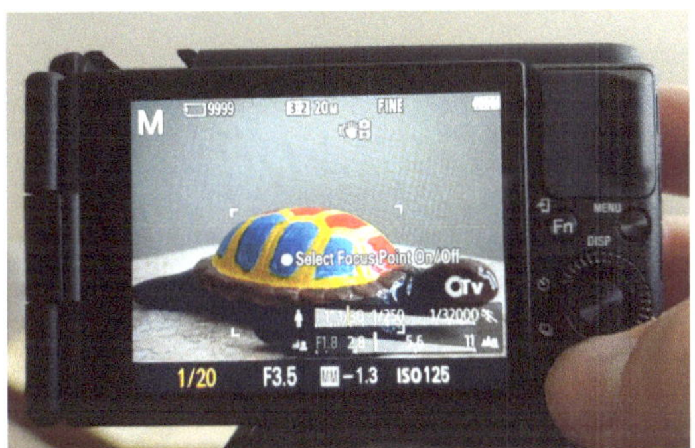

Turtle A. Reid Brown, 2023.

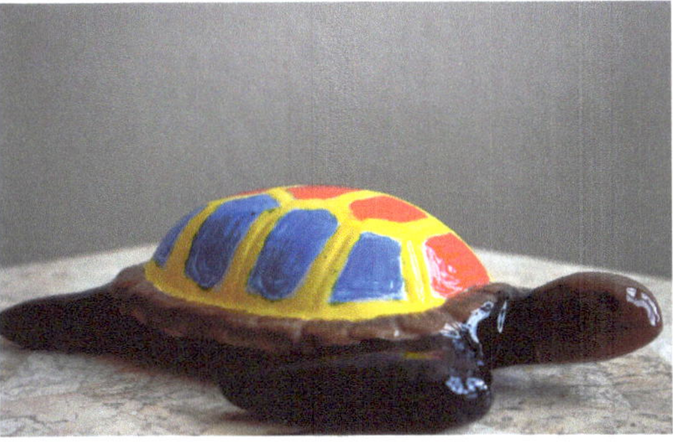

Turtle B. Reid Brown , 2023.

To make a scene blurry and have a small area in focus using a cell phone, observe the pictures below. First, set ISO to auto. Lastly, adjust shutter speed to the exposure that delights you. The scene in the cell phone picture will not be as blurry as using a camera because of my particular cell phones nonadjustable aperture.

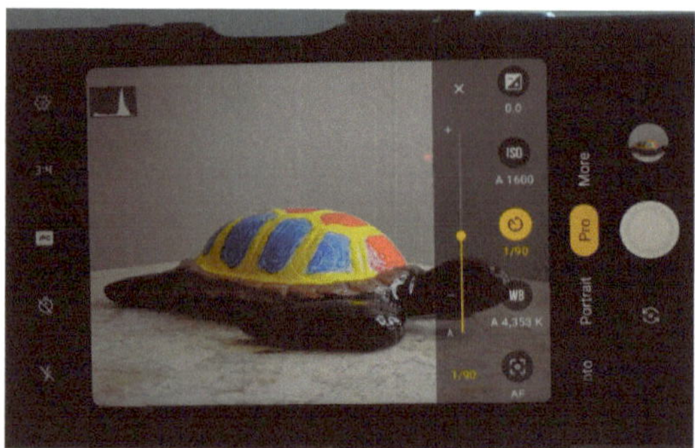

Turtle C. Reid Brown , 2023.

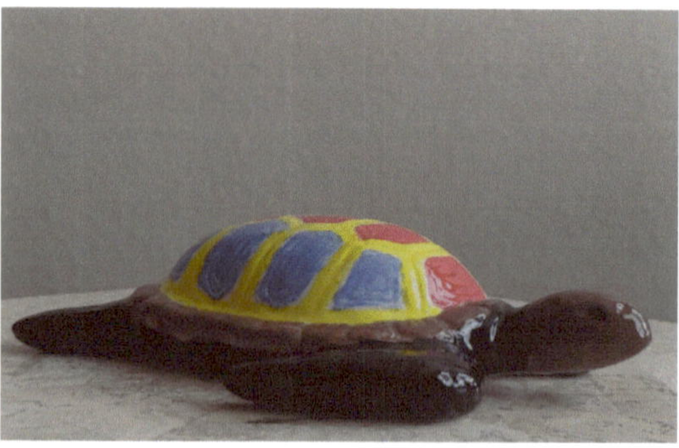

Turtle D. Reid Brown , 2023.

To make a moving subject or elements of design blurry using a camera, observe the pictures below. The element of design I want to make blurry are the water bubbles. First, adjust shutter speed to a lower value (S 1/3) and leave it set. Secondly, adjust aperture to the exposure that you find appealing. For my picture below I liked my aperture set to (F 11). In the bottom picture you can see that the bubbles in the water are blurry from the adjustments I made above.

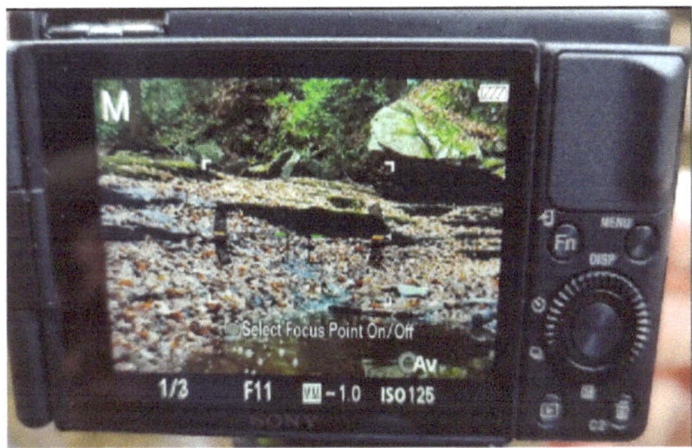

Stream E. Reid Brown, 2023.

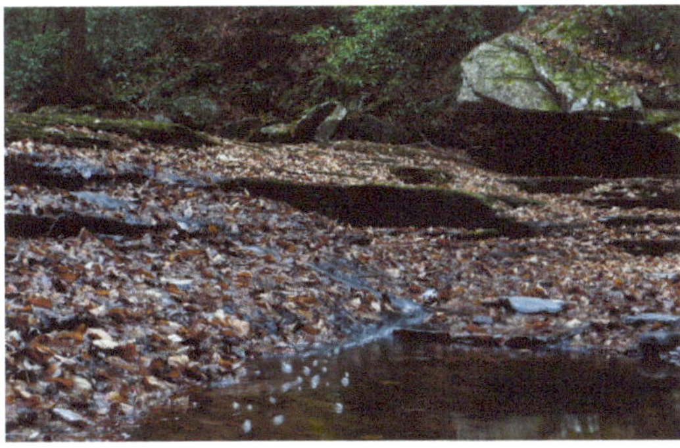

Stream F. Reid Brown , 2023.

To make a moving subject or elements of design blurry using a cell phone, observe the pictures below. The element of design I want to make blurry are the water bubbles. First, set ISO to auto. Secondly, adjust shutter speed to a low value that you care for. For my picture I liked my shutter speed set to (S 1/8).

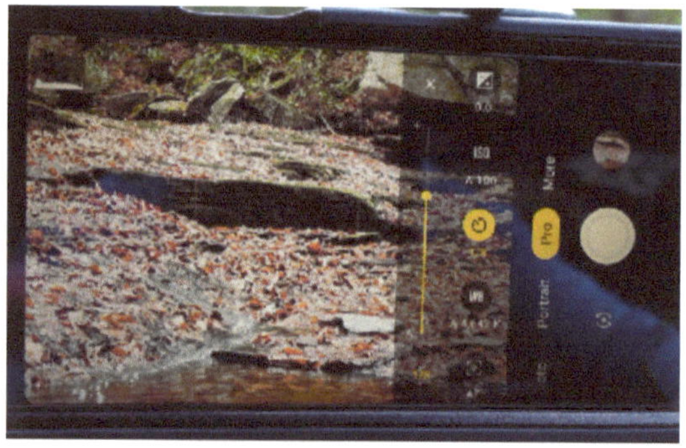

Stream G. Reid Brown , 2023.

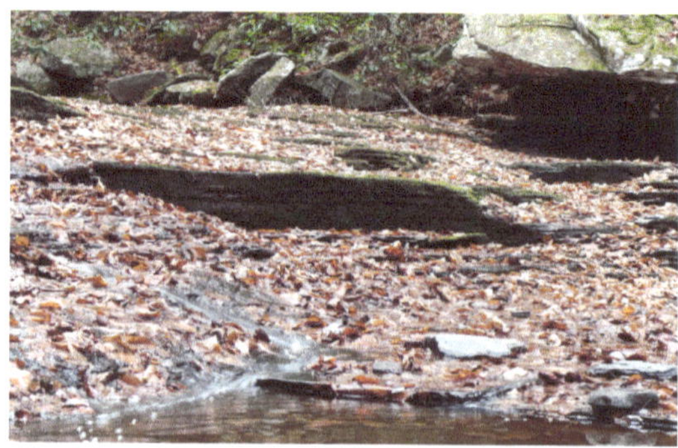

Stream H. Reid Brown , 2023.

To make a moving subject or elements of design be in focus using a camera, observe the pictures below. The element of design I want in focus are the water bubbles. First, adjust shutter speed to a higher value (S 50) and leave it set. Secondly, adjust aperture to the exposure that attracts your artful eye. For my picture below I liked my aperture set to (F 4). In the bottom picture you can see that the bubbles in the water are focused from the adjustments I made above.

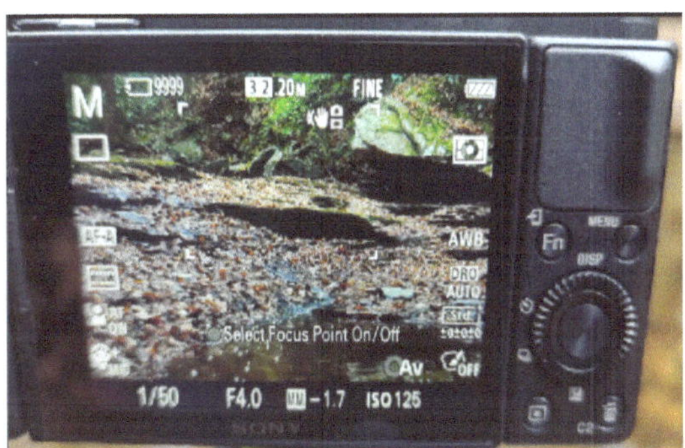

Stream I. Reid Brown, 2023.

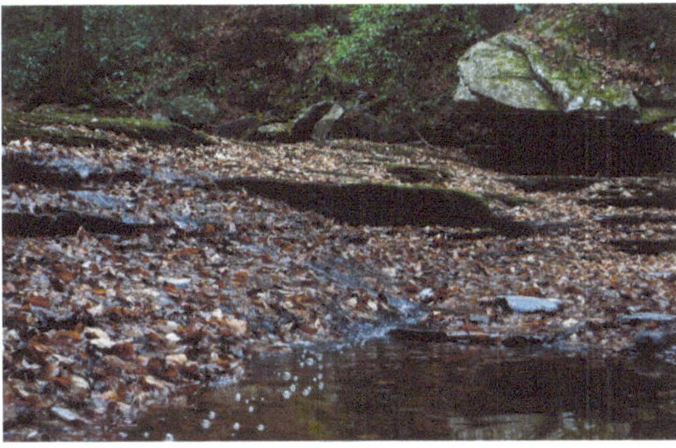

Stream J. Reid Brown , 2023.

To make a moving subject or elements of design be in focus using a cell phone, observe the pictures below. The element of design I want in focus are the water bubbles. First, set ISO to auto. Secondly, adjust shutter speed to a high value that is to your preference. For my picture I liked my shutter speed set to (S 30).

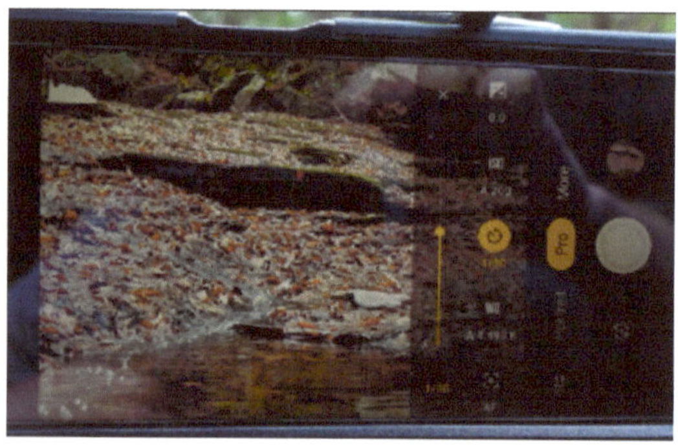

Stream K. Reid Brown , 2023.

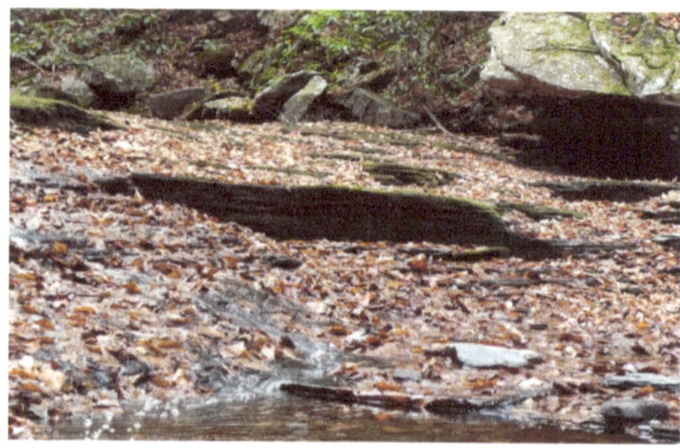

Stream L. Reid Brown , 2023.

Thinking back to your subject and elements of design in your framed scene that you thought about at the beginning of the book. How would you enhance them using the factors of the exposure triangle?

ISO:

____

____

____

Aperture:

____

____

____

Shutter speed:

____

____

____

Don't be discouraged if you don't get the pictures you want right away. Changing ISO, aperture and shutter speed and understanding their relationship in the exposure triangle takes practice, as each scene is unique and different.

I am confident you will gain your footing in time!

Chapter Notes

1. Action Camera Blog. "The Exposure Triangle." Action Camera Blog (blog), February 22, 2017. https://actioncamera.blog/2017/02/22/the-exposure-triangle/.

Capture

It's finally that exciting time to pull out your camera or open your camera app. I encourage you to display the composition assistance grid, to do so go to:

> "Settings" for your camera app or camera. Look for "assistance grid" or "grid" in the display section.

Let's now review what we covered in the previous chapters. Just think, you are now closer to your creative, unique picture taking potential. That's so exciting! On your photography journey, when capturing scenes, I encourage you to take a PICC:

Ponder:
Mentally relax using the look, listen, concentrate technique.

Inspect:
Think about what your subject and supporting elements of design will be. Use the "grid lines" on your camera or phone and the rule of thirds and fill the frame principles to best place them compositionally into your frame so they are artistically pleasing to you and later your viewers.

Change essential settings:
With a compositional idea of how to frame your subject and elements of design ask yourself these questions: Do I want my picture to be in focus across a majority of the scene or to be blurry and have a small area in focus? Is there movement in the scene, will the subject and elements of design be blurry or focused? After answering these questions, adjust the factors of the exposure triangle: ISO, shutter speed and aperture to best highlight your subject and elements of design to your artful liking.

Capture:
With those essential settings set and your subject and elements of design compositionally placed how you would like them in your frame, snap that amazing photograph.

Here is some closing helpful guidance I found through my experiences to enhance your pictures as you take them:

- Take the time to check any recently captured pictures using the camera display screen or phone gallery app. to see if the picture is what you had in mind.

- To get the best color, take pictures in the morning and evening.

- When you want to add more shadows or form element of design, take pictures in the early afternoon when the sun is above you.

- When a landscape is your subject, if you are able, scout out the scene a day or so before taking the picture. This way you can plan what elements of design you want to use in the framed scene.

- The brightest areas of a scene will always attract a viewers eye, try using this to your creative advantage when framing your subject and elements of design in a scene.

- Lastly, when taking pictures of a subject in low light, like early morning or late evening, use a tripod to hold the camera.

In conclusion, I hope the creative process P.I.C.C. has opened your mind, sparked your curiosity, and provided valuable insights on your picture taking journey.

I believe that your thoughts and opinions matter, which is why I encourage you to share a review. By leaving a review, you not only help others discover this book, but also contribute to a community of engaged readers.

So, take a few moments to reflect on your experience and let your voice be heard. Your review might inspire others to start a new and transformative journey in photography. Simply hold your phone camera over the the QR code and click on the link that appears.

Contact the Author

Hold your phone camera over the QR code below, and fill out the form that appears on your phone.

 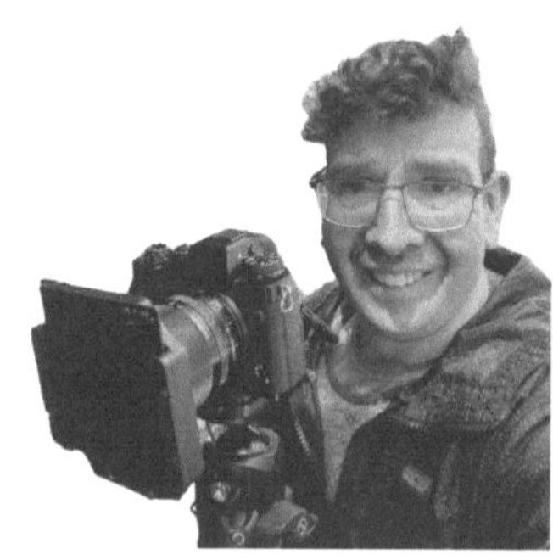

* 9 7 9 8 2 1 8 2 4 4 0 9 5 *